W9-DIH-864

DISCARD

The Library of Explorers and Exploration

JUAN PONCE DE LEÓN

The Exploration of Florida and the Search for the Fountain of Youth

Robert Greenberger

the rosen publishing group's
rosen
central

To Deb, who continues to guide me through times both good and bad

Published in 2003 by The Rosen Publishing Group, Inc.
29 East 21st Street, New York, NY 10010

First Edition

Library of Congress Cataloging-in-Publication Data

Greenberger, Robert.
Juan Ponce de León : the exploration of Florida and the search for the fountain of youth / Robert Greenberger.
    v. cm. — (The library of explorers and exploration)
Includes bibliographical references (p.) and index.
Contents: A man and his legend — Dawn of a new age —
A noble ancestry — Life at sea — Exploring the new world —
Political strife — Land of flowers and fear — A career in twilight —
Florida today — Chronology.
ISBN 0-8239-3627-9 (library bdg.)
1. Ponce de León, Juan, 1460?–1521—Juvenile literature.
2. Explorers—America—Biography—Juvenile literature.
3. Explorers—Spain—Biography—Juvenile literature.
4. America—Discovery and exploration—Spanish—Juvenile literature.
5. Florida—Discovery and exploration—Spanish—Juvenile literature.
[1. Ponce de León, Juan, 1460?–1521. 2. Explorers. 3. America—
Discovery and exploration—Spanish.]
I. Title. II. Series.
E125.P7 G75 2003
972.9'02'092—dc21

                                                    2002003207

Manufactured in the United States of America

CONTENTS

INTRODUCTION

A MAN AND
HIS LEGEND

While most explorers' names bring to mind their individual conquests and discoveries, Juan Ponce de León is most remembered for his search for the legendary Fountain of Youth.

Ponce de León is sometimes even remembered as a fraud, someone who explored in search of a dream. Many people have forgotten how the Iberian soldier helped explore and colonize the island of Puerto Rico. And of all the explorers who came to the New World, it was Ponce de León who lived in closest harmony with the native people and their land.

Juan Ponce de León was a Spanish explorer and conquistador, and the first European to explore Puerto Rico, Florida, the Florida Keys, and parts of Mexico. Many people still wrongly believe that the driving force behind much of Ponce de León's exploration was his desire to find the Fountain of Youth. This mythical fountain supposedly flowed with water that cured illnesses and granted the drinker eternal youth. This statue of the explorer stands beside the San Jose Church in Old San Juan, Puerto Rico.

While myths of a Fountain of Youth existed in the sixteenth century, it was actually furthest from Ponce de León's mind when he set out to find new lands. The image of a crazed sailor hacking through the bush in search of a natural spring is an undeserved legacy for someone who did much to help Europe establish a strong foothold in the New World.

When it was time to explore the mainland of the New World, it was King Ferdinand of the newly unified Spain who asked Ponce de León to begin the search. It led the explorer to find what he named Pascua de Flores, or "Feast of the Flowers," and the first true exploration of North America. Although it's believed that he died before he had confirmed that Florida was not a large island but actually a part of the North American continent, Ponce de León did help locate the Gulf Stream, which forever changed the nature of navigation. Its discovery provided future explorers with a new sea route from the West Indies to Spain.

In the surviving documentation, Ponce de León's history is one that tells the story of a man who had great integrity. He was an intelligent

Spanish explorer Juan Ponce de León searches for the legendary Fountain of Youth on the island of Bimini in this painting from 1513. Bimini is actually two islands northwest of the Bahamas. They extend seven miles and lie about fifty miles east of the Florida coast.

man, one who wanted to do great things for his country, but he was far from an idealist. When duty called, Ponce de León ably served the Crown first as a soldier, then as an explorer, and finally as a pioneer and administrator. It is doubtful that Puerto Rico would have survived as a colony had he not established strategic military posts there and learned to farm its land. Ultimately, Ponce de León was a visionary, a man whose imagination and ambition propelled him as far as he could travel—all the way to the shores of a land untouched by his peers. This is his story.

1

DAWN OF A NEW AGE

After they have been reassured and have lost this fear, they are artless and so free with all they possess, that no one would believe it without having seen it. Of anything they have, if you ask them for it, they never say no; rather they invite the person to share it, and show as much love as if they were giving their hearts; they are content with whatever little thing of whatever kind may be given to them.

—Christopher Columbus, in a 1493 letter to King Ferdinand and Queen Isabella describing his encounters with the Native Americans

Late in the fifteenth century, most of Europe was still a bubbling cauldron of ever-changing boundaries as kingdoms competed for larger territories and power. While monarchies were well established by this time in Germany, England, and France, many other European kingdoms, such as Italy and Portugal, were still searching for ways to increase trade and gain wealth and power. Immense curiosity about what lands lay beyond the sea led to great advances in shipbuilding and navigation in these kingdoms. Monarchs and government leaders understood that whichever territory controlled the best trade routes had an opportunity to reign supreme.

Columbus, sailing under the Spanish flag, sought such trade routes, hoping to find a sea route to Asia. In fact, when Columbus first sailed across the Atlantic Ocean in October 1492, he believed that he had found India. He called the people there Indians, and the West Indies were thus "discovered."

Castile and Aragon

Such discoveries were exactly what were needed in the country now known as Spain. At the time, Spain was several smaller kingdoms united through royal marriage. Much of what we know of Spanish culture traces its roots back over 3,000 years to the Iberian Peninsula. During that time, the Phoenicians, the Greeks, the Celts, the Carthaginians, and the Romans cultivated the lands. In each case, they left behind a permanent addition to the peninsula, shaping its language, economy, and culture.

By AD 711, the arrival of the Moors (Muslims), in that region had altered its political landscape. Originally invited from North Africa to assist King Witiza's supporters in a civil war, the Moors settled

Italian navigator Christopher Columbus was among the first Europeans to explore the New World. His four voyages, 1492–1493, 1493–1496, 1498–1500, and 1502–1504, led the way for European exploration, exploitation, and colonization of these new lands. This painting depicts Columbus taking possession of San Salvador on October 12, 1492.

This map from the 1400s depicts the Iberian Peninsula, home to Spain and Portugal in southwestern Europe. The peninsula's name is thought to come from its ancient inhabitants, whom the Greeks called Iberians after the Iberus, the peninsula's second longest river. The Pyrenees mountain chain in the northeast separates the peninsula from the rest of Europe, and the Strait of Gibraltar separates it from North Africa.

in the area. They did so for religious reasons, but also because they wanted to find the truth to the legend of King Solomon's treasures, which were believed to be near the city of Toledo.

Over the next several centuries, one generation after another attempted to conquer portions of the land, setting up a series of small kingdoms. By the fifteenth century, however, these small kingdoms had more or less formed two major countries: Castile and Aragon. Portugal, also on the peninsula, shared much of this history but managed to control a consistent territory for longer stretches of time. This enabled its culture to remain more unchanged than those of the neighboring lands.

By the late 1400s, Castile's 800-year effort to expel the Moors from Spain, called the Reconquest, was nearing completion. Castile was adjusting to its new rulers, Queen Isabella I and her husband King Ferdinand V, after two decades of chaotic leadership under her half brother Enrique IV. A brief civil war broke out upon Enrique's death, but it became obvious that the people preferred Isabella to Enrique's daughter, Juana, who was not a popular choice. As a result, other countries did not support Juana's leadership. The Treaty of Alcacovas neatly divided ownership of both land and sea between the kingdom of Castile and Portugal (Enrique's homeland).

This detail of an Islamic/Spanish fresco depicts the Christian conquest of Mallorca, the largest of the Balearic Islands in the western Mediterranean Sea. Christian knights in chainmail suits surround James the Conqueror, king of Aragon, as he prepares to attack the island.

Such was the political landscape when Columbus arrived before the Crown in search of a patron for his Enterprise of the Indies. The Portuguese government was uninterested in his plan to reach Asia at the time, and a frustrated Columbus instead sought support in Castile.

The year of the Treaty of Alcacovas, 1479, also saw the death of Aragon's King Juan II. Isabella became Isabella I of Castile and Ferdinand adopted the title Ferdinand II of Aragon. This effectively gave the couple control of both countries. But rather

15

When Ferdinand II succeeded to the crown of Aragon in 1479, Ferdinand and Isabella *(above)* became the second most powerful monarchs in Europe after the Valois of France. Juan II of Aragon arranged the 1469 marriage of his son and heir, Ferdinand, with Isabella of Castile for tactical reasons: He needed Castilian support against French aggression in the Pyrenees.

than unite them, they chose to rule them as entirely separate lands.

By January 1492, the Reconquest was complete, and the Crown was now available to consider other matters, including establishing new trade routes. If nothing else, it provided a new task for the kingdom's conquistadors, or soldiers. The Crown finally approved Christopher Columbus's petition to seek out new routes to the East by sailing west.

Columbus's first voyage in 1492 was deemed a success. Within a month of his triumphant return to Europe the following year, Columbus was already assembling a second, much larger expedition. Thousands of men, hungry to gain skills as successful mariners, longed to join the now famous explorer. Columbus's second transatlantic journey would encompass seventeen vessels and hundreds of crewmen, including 200 gentlemen not on the royal payroll. Among those was a young man named Juan Ponce de León, who must have felt very lucky indeed.

2

A NOBLE ANCESTRY

Juan Ponce [de León] was a poor squire when he came here [to Española], and in Spain he had been a servant of Pedro Nuñez de Guzman, brother of Ramirez Nuñez, Lord of Toral. This same Pedro Nuñez, when Juan Ponce served him as a page, did not have 100,000 maravedis or thereabouts of income, despite the fact that he was of illustrious blood and later the tutor of the Very Serene Lord Prince Don Fernando, who now is king of the Romans.

—Nicolas Oviedo, *General and Natural History of the Indies*, 1508

Juan Ponce de León y Figueroa was born in the village of Tierra de Campos Palencia, in what is today known as the province of Valladolid, Spain, on the banks of the Valderaduey River. His year of birth, often disputed by historians, was likely between 1460 and 1474.

This is a map of Spain. Spain's northwestern city of Valladolid, where Juan Ponce de León was born, has a colorful history. Catholic monarchs Queen Isabella and King Ferdinand were married there in 1469, and Christopher Columbus died there in 1506. Besides its many gothic-styled landmarks, Valladolid also houses one of Spain's oldest universities, which was founded in 1346.

Bay of Biscay

Coruña
Castropol
Gijón
Santander
Santiago
Oviedo
Bilbao
Lugo
San Sebastián
Vitoria
León
Pamp
Orense
Vigo
edra
Túy
Río Miño
Río Isla
Río Pisuerga
Palencia
Burgos
Logroño
Aranda de Duero
Soria
Valladolid
Calat
Zamora
Río Duero
Río Douro
Segovia
Salamanca
Ávila
Tajo
Madrid
Guadalajara
Portugal
Cuenca
Toledo
Tarancón
Tajo
Cáceres
Río Júcar
Río
Guardiana
Ciudad Real
Albacete
Badajoz
Mérida
Guadalimar
Río Segura
Linares
Murcia
Guadalquivir
Córdoba
Jaén
Seville
Ayamonte
Huelva
Granada
Genil
Río
Almería
Golfo de Cádiz
Antequera
Jerez de la Frontera
Cadiz
Málaga
Gibraltar (U.K.)
Algeciras
Isla de Alborán (Spain)
Atlantic
Strait of Gibraltar
Ceuta (Sp.)
Ocean
Morocco
Melilla

A Royal Marriage

Given the incomplete records and changing customs of the era, it is hard to properly trace Ponce de León's ancestry. It is clear, however, that there was noble blood among his family members. He was descended from an ancient and royal family; his surname was acquired through the marriage of one of the Ponces to Doña Aldonza de León, daughter of Alfonso IX. His father was Pedro, Fourth Lord of Villagarcia, and his mother was Dona Leónor de Figueroa, daughter to Lorenzo Suarez de Figueroa and Maria Manuel. Some records indicate that his parents died young, and that Ponce de León was raised by a great-aunt.

It is known that he was one of three brothers, his siblings being Fray Pedro and Luis. As an adult, Luis was named first marquis of Zahara and fifth lord of Villagarcia. He married Francisca, marquesa de Cadiz, likely his second cousin. Her father was Rodrigo de León, duke and marquis of Cadiz, a prosperous bay region. Fray Pedro was given the title knight commander of the Sovereign Order of Malta.

Rodrigo de León was considered the major factor in Granada's victory over the remaining Moors in the final years of the Reconquest. As a result, he was decorated by the Crown and given many titles and privileges, enhancing the Ponce de León family's overall royal prestige.

The Spanish explorer Juan Ponce de León is featured in this engraving from 1728. As a teenager, he joined Spanish forces that eventually defeated the Moors of Granada, and in 1493, he accompanied Christopher Columbus on his second voyage to America. Later, he conquered the island of Puerto Rico and served as its governor, winning fame and fortune as well as royal support.

Ponce de León's great-grandfather, also named Pedro, was known as the count of Medellin and first count of Arcos. The second and third counts of Arcos were also members of the family—great-uncle Juan and nephew Rodrigo, named after the war hero. The paternal grandmother, Doña Teresa Ponce de León y Guzman, was known as La Señora de la Casa Toral.

It was this connection with the House of Toral and Guzman side of the family that led young Ponce de León to be assigned as squire to Don Pedro Nuñez de Guzman, knight commander of the Order of Calatrava. For five years, he trained under the older soldier and fought in the conflicts with the Moors.

When the Reconquest was over and the Spanish Moors were forced from Granada, Ponce de León left Don Pedro's employ and went to Cadiz, one of the oldest cities in western Europe. He may have been in his late teenage years when he arrived in Cadiz, finished with fighting and ready to begin a new life.

What he discovered there surprised and excited him. Seventeen ships were being readied for Columbus's second trip to the New World.

Christopher Columbus is shown at the Port of Palos preparing to leave for his first voyage on August 3, 1492, in this nineteenth-century painting by Ricardo Balaca. On this trip Columbus journeyed to the Bahamas, Cuba, and Hispaniola, inspiring many young would-be explorers, including Ponce de León.

The respected explorer was in a hurry, fearing a confrontation between King João II of Portugal and Queen Isabella. Clearly Columbus's discovery for Spain was in violation of the Treaty of Alcacovas, and he needed to return to the New World and further establish Spain's presence before a Portuguese ship could do so. It finally took an order from Pope Alexander VI to relocate the boundaries established in the treaty, removing the Portuguese threat.

There is no record of how Ponce de León managed passage on the voyage. He had little money, so it may have been one of his older relatives who helped pay his way or arranged for him to be among the 200 volunteers. Regardless, he was chosen. When the ships departed on October 4, 1493, to cross the Atlantic Ocean, Ponce de León was most likely anticipating what would soon become one of the greatest wonders of his lifetime: He was ready to cast his eyes upon the lands of the New World.

3

LIFE AT SEA

They put us in a tiny chamber that was three palms high and five palms square, in which, as we entered, the force of the sea did such violence to our stomachs and heads, that, parents and children, old and young, we turned the color of corpses, and we commenced to give up our souls.

—Eugenio de Salazar, 1573

Life at sea had changed very little for hundreds of years. Documents through the ages attest to the difficult life between ports. Forceful winds, wretched weather, rationed food, confined quarters, thirst, disease, and death were commonplace at sea. Eugenio de Salazar's 1573 account must have been similar to the conditions nearly a century earlier. Despite the difficult nature of sailing across the Atlantic Ocean, however, thousands of men and boys, especially those seeking great riches, wanted to be a part of Columbus's crew. Not surprisingly, Ponce de León was one of these men.

Rhythm and Timing

Eugenio de Salazar described the various watches that formed the day. The sand-filled half-hour glass, or *ampolleta*, often clogged during humid weather but helped determine the distance sailed and was tended to by a succession of boys. They had to be exact in their timing of turning the glass in order to keep track of the distance that was sailed. Spares were usually kept, too, since these precision-made tools were fragile. The boys would call out the change of watch, alerting the crew when they could rest, eat, or work. They usually did so with chants or songs reflecting the mood of the day. The language also seemed to include prayers, denoting the large role that religion played in sailors' lives. The four-hour watches on Columbus's journey were changed at 4:00, 8:00, and 12:00, both day and night.

Frequent praying by the crew was normal. On this particular voyage, Friar Bernardo Buil—credited as the first man to recite mass in the New World—and a dozen Benedictine monks were brought along to help convert the pagan natives to Catholicism. This was one of the main objectives of Columbus's second journey, in addition to colonizing new lands.

Benedictine monks are praying with Saint Benedict in this image. Saint Benedict (AD 480–547) was the founder of Western monk society. He laid down monastic foundations that ushered in a tradition of learning and artistic achievement that influenced all of northwestern Europe. Because of the subsequent work monks did to spread the word of the Catholic Church in many European countries, in 1964 Pope Paul VI proclaimed Benedict the patron saint of all of Europe.

An hourglass consists of two glass chambers and a fixed quantity of sand that trickles from one chamber to the other in a predetermined and fixed amount of time. Since hourglasses are sealed and largely unaffected by heat, cold, and swinging about, they have a long history of use at sea. There are records of hourglasses in ships' inventories from AD 1400. This type of hourglass was used on board English ships of the eighteenth century.

Columbus, admiral of the Ocean Sea, and viceroy and governor of the islands that he had "discovered," was instructed by the Castilian monarchy to treat the Indians "very well and lovingly"—behavior for which Ponce de León would be remembered much later.

Sunrise concluded the boys' shift of keeping watch, turning the half-hour glass, and ensuring that the decks were kept clean. Men slept wherever there was space, for there was little to be found, and the odors aboard the ship were extraordinarily strong. Sailors normally had only one set of clothing that they wore until it was ragged.

During the shift changes, the navigator reported his course to the incoming watch captain and new navigator. Each crew member would then repeat the course, to avoid errors. After all, the slightest deviation from the bearing could send a ship hundreds of miles off course. The remaining crew members pumped the ship dry, watched the sails, performed repairs, scrubbed the rails, and tended to other matters of maintenance.

The night crews were smaller, consisting of men who sometimes washed clothing in buckets of salt water, swapped tall tales, and mended fishing lines. In fact, Columbus and his crew were a clean lot; swimming in the calmer oceans and at every river stop, and washing themselves and their clothes—very unusual behavior for fifteenth-century voyages.

Desperate Conditions

On the second voyage, Juan Rodriguez de Fonseca, the archdeacon of Seville, was charged with outfitting each of Columbus's seventeen vessels. He bought substandard supplies and materials, pocketing the difference and grabbing a hefty profit for himself. As a result, wooden barrels of wine were so poorly made that much of the precious liquid leaked out or spoiled.

Life aboard fifteenth-century ships was difficult and dangerous. The sailors ate poorly and often suffered from scurvy from the lack of vitamin C. The ships were cramped with people and provisions, and these conditions contributed to the spread of illness and disease. Many sailors also suffered from seasickness, and as a result, the decks were often covered with human waste.

The crew had probably one hot meal per day. Because there was no official cook on board, it is presumed by historians that boys not watching the glass took turns cooking over a cookbox on deck or in an enclosed room below deck on larger vessels. All meals included hardtack, or sea biscuits, which were wheat flour–based crackers baked in large quantities before each voyage. Breakfast usually consisted of a small amount of cheese, some garlic, and sardines.

Columbus described the food on his voyage in a letter to the sovereigns: "Victualling [supplying them with food] should be done in this manner: . . . the breadstuff to be good biscuit, well-seasoned and not old, or the major portion will be wasted . . . Further there will be wanted wine, salt meat, oil, vinegar, cheese, chickpeas, lentils, beans, salt fish and fishing tackle, honey, rice, almonds, and raisins."

Little was known then about proper nutrition, so scurvy, caused by a vitamin C deficiency, was common on all long voyages. As a result, many sailors faced poor health with symptoms that included bleeding gums, fever, pain, weakness, and even death.

Luckily for Ponce de León, Columbus's second voyage benefited from good weather. Their first stop was the Canary Islands on October 11, where they gathered additional supplies. Three days later, they made port at Gomera for final repairs before committing to the long transatlantic crossing. Along the way, Ponce de León, who was already trained as a soldier, learned how to become a useful sailor.

Based on primary resources available to us, such as Salazar's letter, life at sea was hardest on the passengers, like Ponce de León, who were often seasick. The decks below were often wet with waste or slick and slippery with seawater.

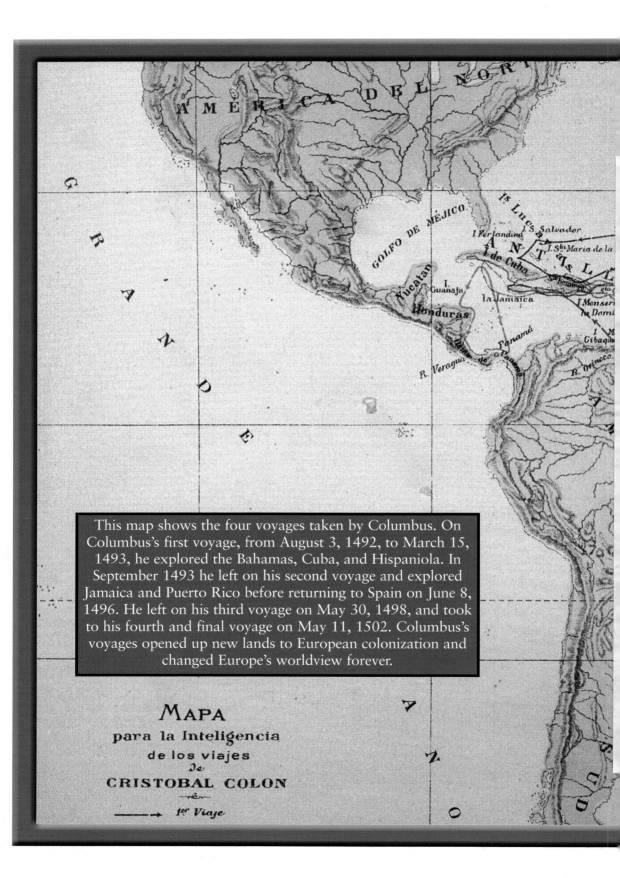

This map shows the four voyages taken by Columbus. On Columbus's first voyage, from August 3, 1492, to March 15, 1493, he explored the Bahamas, Cuba, and Hispaniola. In September 1493 he left on his second voyage and explored Jamaica and Puerto Rico before returning to Spain on June 8, 1496. He left on his third voyage on May 30, 1498, and took to his fourth and final voyage on May 11, 1502. Columbus's voyages opened up new lands to European colonization and changed Europe's worldview forever.

MAPA
para la Inteligencia
de los viajes
de
CRISTOBAL COLON

⟶ 1er Viaje

OCÉ...

l'Ázores.

Salamanca
Madrid
Lisboa R. Tajo
Sevilla Córdoba
Baza
Granada
Pto de Palos
Argel Túnez
COSTA DE MARRUECOS
Fez

1er Viaje (vuelta)

Iª Canarias

(ida)
(vuelta)
3ª Viaje (vuelta)
2º Viaje (vuelta)
2º Viaje (ida)
Guadalupe
4º Viaje (ida)
Iª del Cabo Verde
S. Luis
3r Viaje (ida.)
...dad

OCÉANO

ÁFRICA

Nexo

S. Luis
Sierra Leona

Amazono

ATLÁNTICO

The passengers counted on a guardian to protect their meager belongings while they accepted
food rations from a dispenser. It was impossible to
avoid the odor of sickness in the cramped space.
Any available room on the ships was filled to
capacity, for, in addition to enough provisions to
sustain the crew and passengers for months,
Columbus also carried enough seeds, plants, animals, and tools to establish the new colony.
(Historians reported that sailors overcrowded
every ship, with a total of 1,200 being sent to the
New World when the seventeen ships were only
meant to handle a combined total of 1,000.)

At last, land was sighted on Sunday, November
10, and the island was named Dominica, which is
Latin for "Sunday." Four islands were spotted in
all, and the following day the fleet landed at what
is now Guadeloupe. From there, Columbus and
his explorers found and named numerous islands
until, on November 27, they found one that the
native Taino Indians called Borinquen. Columbus
called it San Juan Bautista, or St. John the Baptist.
Today we know it as Puerto Rico.

4

EXPLORING THE NEW WORLD

And since [Ponce de León] had been a captain during the conquest of Higüey [Hispanola], he had information from that province and he wanted to know from the Indians who on the island of Borinquen or San Juan had a lot of gold.
—Nicolas Oviedo, *General and Natural History of the Indies*, 1508

Columbus quickly left San Juan Bautista, or Puerto Rico, preferring to determine the status of his first colony, La Navidad. He had founded La Navidad on Hispaniola, and he wanted to learn the progress of the crewmen he had left behind from his previous voyage. During that journey, the *Santa Maria* was abandoned after she ran aground, so nearly four dozen people remained to form the first European foothold in the New World. But when Columbus's new fleet returned to the island, the colony was gone and its inhabitants were dead.

The expedition then sailed forty miles east and founded the second colony, La Isabela. (Later it was rebuilt into Nueva Isabela and was finally named Santo Domingo in 1495.)

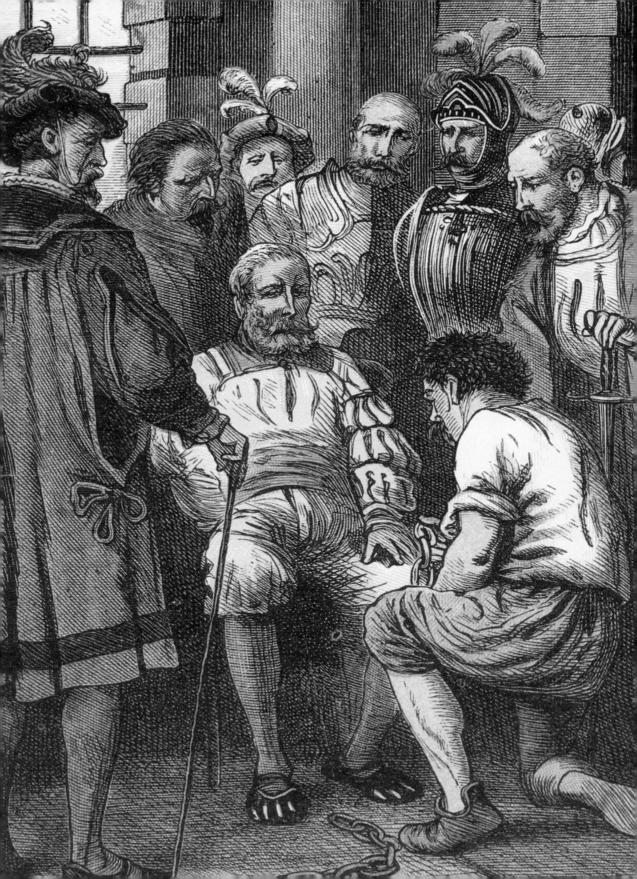

From this point in history, the whereabouts of Ponce de León become obscure. There is little surviving documentation to indicate what he did between 1493 and 1502. Most historians seem to believe that when Columbus dispatched a ship back to Castile, Ponce de León was one of its crew members. Still, what he did in Europe for nearly a decade is a mystery.

Ponce de León's name surfaces again, however, on the roster of a ship returning to the New World in 1502. In the intervening years, Columbus and his crews attempted to colonize Hispaniola, but failed at successfully farming European grains. The local environment did not help, nor did European arrogance, which led to distrust between the natives and the colonists.

The disgruntled settlers had staged a revolt against Columbus and would no longer accept him as governor. Their discontent, along with a lack of gold and spices to send back to the Spanish Crown, brought Columbus's hold on the region into question. The Spanish monarchy ordered Francisco de Bobadilla to sail west as the new royal commissioner and to investigate charges against the explorer.

Because the colonists of Santo Domingo lodged so many complaints against Columbus, Castile sent men to return him to Spain. Francisco de Bobadilla arrived on August 23, 1500, and seized control of the settlement. In October, he sent Columbus home in chains, as is illustrated in this image.

Paradise Lost

The newly empowered Bobadilla arrived in Santo Domingo in 1500 and was appalled at what he found there. There were great conflicts among the colonists, who were now living in a total state of rebellion. Bobadilla immediately set about putting things in order, but his system was harsh. His cruel methods caused Columbus to be sent back to Castile in chains. This public outrage meant Bobadilla had to be replaced. Don Fray Nicolás de Ovando was sent to take his place in February 1502. Ovando, knight commander of Lares, took thirty-two ships with him to bring order to the chaos that was Spain's newest colony. But he first had to survive the journey when a freak storm scattered his vessels, sinking one of them.

When he arrived, he quickly took control of the unruly colony and restored dignity to the Columbus name and holdings. Columbus's gold was placed on one of the twenty-eight ships sched-uled to return to Europe, along with the newly unemployed Bobadilla.

At the same time, Columbus was already outfit-ted for his fourth and final journey to the New World. The Spanish Crown forbade him to anchor at Hispaniola, but he did so anyway, seek-ing to avoid a storm he sensed was brewing. He wound up riding out the bad weather anchored some fifty miles west of Santo Domingo.

Bobadilla's fateful convoy of ships ignored the turn in weather, though, and paid a high price: Only the ship bearing Columbus's gold made it safely to Europe; three others returned to Hispaniola. The remaining twenty-four vessels were lost at sea, with their crews presumed dead, including Bobadilla.

Tensions Mount

The Taino Indians who inhabited Hispaniola were relatively peaceful and usually did not mind sharing their land with the Europeans. They were thought to have numbered 30,000, but their population dropped dramatically over the next two decades.

Ovando discovered that tensions between the natives, who were known as Indians, and the colonists were increasing daily. Skirmishes and fights had broken out, which reduced the colony's ability to farm the land or mine it for gold. For two years, Ovando tried to fortify the settlements and subdue the natives. His method of pacification, however, meant outright murder.

Higüey was located in the easternmost region of the island of Hispaniola and was seen as the area with the most conflict. Legend has it that a Castilian's dog killed a Taino Indian and there was a retaliatory strike that left eight Europeans dead. Governor Ovando, who needed the situation settled once and for all, dispatched Juan de Esquivel to conquer the region.

In 1503, Esquivel succeeded with superior firepower. The Tainos were silenced. Their leader, Cortubano, managed to escape and subsequently attacked the Europeans from time to time. Although vanquished, the Tainos refused to offer a tribute (taxes) in the form of their beloved cassava bread.

Esquivel formed a small garrison, or military post, and removed most of his troops. The men who remained immediately began abusing the Tainos. Finally, having had enough of the poor treatment, the Tainos fought back and, in 1504, attacked the garrison and burned it to the ground.

Ovando, who considered this attack an act of war, ordered Esquivel to fight back. Four hundred men were assembled for this task, and Ponce de León, the former soldier, was now a lieutenant who led the forces from Santo Domingo.

An eyewitness account states that the Europeans were outnumbered by the Indians by four to one, but the well-trained conquistadors defeated them anyway. Many were killed, but others were captured and used as part of the growing slave trade between the New World and Europe. The troops even managed to find the former Taino chief, Cortubano, and return him to Santo Domingo. He was tried and found guilty, and eventually hanged for his crimes.

Growing tensions between the settlers and the Tainos led the Europeans to attack the native peoples. With their superior firepower, the Europeans killed many of the Tainos and enslaved most of the rest.

The remaining members of the tribes stayed behind as slaves or escaped to neighboring islands. Of those who were enslaved, several killed their children in order to spare them from the cruelties of the settlers while others committed suicide. Over time, this led the conquistadors to actively seek out any remaining Taino Indians and bring them back. Within one decade, the proud Indian nation of 30,000 was reduced to less than 4,000 people.

The Fertile Lands of Salvaleon

Ponce de León, who showed great courage during the conflict in Hispaniola, was rewarded with an *encomienda* (land grant) located on the Yuma River, and he was assigned a number of Indians (called a *repartimiento*) to work its fields. With Esquivel leaving for Jamaica, Ovando named Ponce de León *delantado*, or frontier governor of the province.

Suddenly possessing what is believed to have been approximately 225 acres of land, Ponce de León set to work farming yucca, sweet potatoes, and vegetables, and raising pigs, cattle, and horses. It's uncertain how he learned to be a farmer, but he seemed to be exceptionally talented at the task. In a very short time, he managed to raise enough yucca to start baking it into cassava bread on an ongoing basis. As a result, when ships stopped at the Bay of Yuma for supplies,

European settlers were often very cruel to the native peoples of the lands they were colonizing. Although Ponce de León was also interested in colonizing the New World, he was more of a victim than a victimizer. Despite his political disputes, he continued to find support from the Spanish Crown.

they would load up on his bread, which remained fresh longer and better than the hardtack.

Not only was Ponce de León an excellent farmer, he was a natural diplomat. Even though he technically owned the slaves, he treated them fairly and, as a result, they worked hard. Few other colonists mirrored this approach, but a notable exception was Vasco Nuñez de Balboa, who was Ponce de León's good friend. Balboa had a similar spread of land, but his was in a less desirable area in what is now Haiti. Moreover, it left him bankrupt.

43

In contrast, Ponce de León built up a sizeable fortune even without mining for gold. His personal wealth also increased when he married Leónor, the daughter of a Santo Domingo innkeeper. The exact date of this union is unrecorded, but over the following years the couple had four children: Juana, Isabel, Maria, and Luis. It should be noted that Leónor was European, so their New World marriage gave Ponce de León additional respect. At the time, being European-born was a critical factor in both politics and society.

Ponce de León continued to impress Governor Ovando so much that, in 1505, he was given the charge of establishing a new colony, the island's sixteenth. Ponce de León selected a site near his land and named it Salvaleon, after his maternal grandmother. He constructed a huge home on his new land some twenty miles from Higüey, where it still stands today.

5

POLITICAL STRIFE

And learning that, he communicated in secret with the Knight Commander who at that time resided in Española; who gave him permission to pass to the island of San Juan to explore and learn what it was like.
—Nicolas Oviedo, *General and Natural History of the Indies,* 1508

During the expansion and development of Hispaniola, life back in Spain was getting tumultuous. Queen Isabella died on November 26, 1504. And, because the heir to her throne, her daughter Juana, was considered insane, it took more than a few years for the new ruler to be agreed upon. Isabella's husband, Ferdinand, ruled as regent for a short time before Juana's husband, Felipe, tried to keep things in order on behalf of his wife. When Felipe died in September 1506, however, there was no way Juana could rule on her own. Ferdinand was asked to return from Naples, Italy, and resume power in 1507.

San Juan Bautista

On May 3, 1505, the Spanish Crown had appointed Vicente Yanez Pinzon as captain of San Juan Bautista. Previously, he had captained the *Niña* on Columbus's first voyage and was somewhat familiar with the area. Not a particularly skilled colonist, he failed to accomplish anything of merit during his two-year grant.

Complicating matters, Columbus had an agreement that made him the sole governor of the island despite Pinzon, which succeeded any other decision. And complicating matters further, when Columbus died in 1506, his son Diego began a bitter campaign to retain all of his father's rights and holdings, including those in the New World.

On Santo Domingo, Ponce de León learned a great deal by speaking with natives who continued to cross from area islands and from fellow colonists who anchored nearby for supplies. He had heard of the troubles on San Juan Bautista and

A knight kneels before King Ferdinand II in this image from 1492. Not only did Ferdinand send explorers out to claim the New World for Spain, but he consolidated Spanish power throughout Europe. He also instituted the Spanish Inquisition, which bolstered religious and political unity among Catholics by punishing and murdering Jews (and later Muslims). Under Ferdinand, the power of the monarchy grew, the power of parliament was curbed, and the Catholic Church became an instrument of politics. During his reign, Spain became a maritime power and revolutionized European commerce. The leadership of King Ferdinand and Queen Isabella had a great impact on the history of the world as well as that of Spain.

was keeping up on the island's local politics. Records indicate that he first visited the area on July 1, 1506, landing his five ships in the very same spot as Columbus had done in 1493. The location, known then as El Aguada, was one of the best spots for fresh water. Gonzalo Fernandez de Oviedo y Valdes speculated that Ponce de León scouted the island initially to broaden his own financial interests. It was his belief that Ponce de León was prompted by his own curiosity and visited to learn exactly how much gold was available to be mined.

In fact, Oviedo believed that Ponce de León secretly worked with Hispaniola's Governor Ovando to gain permission to explore the island. Juan Gonzalez Ponce de León, a first cousin, served as Ponce de León's interpreter with the Taino natives. Together, and with approximately 100 other men, they began an effort to colonize San Juan Bautista.

Guaybana, a cacique or chief, whose mother was well aware of the Spanish, led the Tainos. He was counseled by his mother to be hospitable and he befriended Ponce de León and his men. There were dances known as *arietos*, much food, and other provisions in honor of the Europeans. The conquistadors also witnessed *batos*, or ball games. As was the custom of the Taino, Guaybana and Ponce de León even

Christopher Columbus with his sons Diego and Hernando. After Columbus died, his sons claimed the New World territory, including San Juan Bautista.

briefly swapped names. The chief even went so far as to offer his sister to Ponce de León in marriage, but the explorer declined.

Ponce de León's first act had Juan Gonzalez leading a group of men overland eighty-five miles to what is now the city of San Juan. The Taino Indians had indicated there was a better place for a port, and Ponce de León wanted to explore the area. The men scouted the site, and that fall brought back samples of the land to check them for gold.

Caparra

With positive news, Ponce de León ordered that the five ships immediately set sail for the new port while he explored the terrain. It took the conquistadors eight days to cover the distance by foot, while the boats made it in one day. They decided to build a settlement about ten miles from the current city. Although it could not be officially recognized until the king authorized its establishment, that did not stop Ponce de León. They named the settlement Caparra (later named Ciudad de Puerto Rico) after the Roman town of Capera, and it was built that winter.

By all accounts the settlement was a huge mistake. Simply stated, Caparra was a hill surrounded by a swamp, which meant it was not safe to farm or easy to protect. Oviedo's records showed that he thought everyone living in Caparra looked sickly; they fell victim to poor health as a result of conditions that he believed were caused by the contaminated and silt-laden swamp water.

Guaybana further helped Ponce de León and his men by showing them where to find gold, which the Taino used for jewelry. To the Native Americans it held no value. When the gold was smelted, however, it was judged inferior to the metal found on the island of Hispaniola, but good enough for King Ferdinand.

On the north coast of Puerto Rico, Ponce de León found a well-protected bay that could harbor many sailing vessels; on high ground beside the bay he founded Caparra, the island's first town and mining and agricultural site. By 1521, the town was moved to an islet at the northern end of the harbor and renamed Puerto Rico, or "Rich Port." Through time and common usage the port became known as San Juan while the name Puerto Rico applied to the whole island.

A Secret Mission

After establishing Caparra, Ponce de León and most of the men returned back to Higüey, resuming their normal lives and routines.

Politically, this was a secret mission, one undertaken by Ponce de León and Ovando because they recognized Pinzon would not fulfill his commission and the rulers of Castile were still settling issues of royal succession. Confusing matters further was Columbus's death and his son's claims to the New World territory, including San Juan Bautista.

The next eighteen months passed smoothly as Ponce de León governed wisely and his fortunes as a farmer grew. His family expanded, too. Everyone seemed content but Ponce de León, who had not let San Juan Bautista stray far from his mind. In the spring of 1508, he formally applied to the Crown for permission to mount an expedition of the island. And by August, he had invested his money in a ship with fifty men and made the first official trip there.

He sailed to his first stop, Euancia, on August 19 before landing at San Juan Bay. Caparra had been abandoned early in 1507, but Ponce de León restored order there and added more buildings. He used his successful experiences on Higüey to guide his construction efforts, building another bakery to turn the yucca into cassava bread for sale to passing ships. The profits would later help fund his excavation efforts as his search for gold increased.

Control, Claims, and Confusion

Ponce de León reported to Santo Domingo in April 1509, and made a presentation to Governor Ovando about San Juan Bautista. By May 11, a formal contract had been drawn authorizing him to further develop the land. Like preceding agreements, this was also a secret deal between King

Ferdinand, Governor Ovando, Ponce de León, royal treasurer Miguel de Pasamonte, and chief justice Alonso Maldonado.

As expected, Diego Columbus returned to the New World that July and reclaimed his father's titles and privileges. These included being installed as governor of all Spanish possessions in the West Indies and being named first admiral. However, the courts clearly directed Diego to exclude San Juan Bautista, despite the fact that the island was clearly a Columbus discovery. Diego, although displeased, shrewdly named Ponce de León his deputy, allowing Ponce to act as governor of San Juan Bautista anyway, in addition to retaining control over Higüey on Hispaniola.

Unknown to Diego, and even to Ponce de León and Ovando, King Ferdinand had already formally appointed Ponce de León governor of San Juan Bautista on August 23, 1509.

Moreover, an aristocrat named Don Cristobal de Sotomayor arrived in the New World with Diego and claimed that the king had promised him governorship of the island. This claim rapidly vanished, however, once Ponce de León named Sotomayor as his lieutenant.

After the confusion was settled, Ponce de León returned to Salvaleon and restocked for an extended stay on San Juan Bautista. It was on this trip that he brought his wife and four children with him to their new home. It was also that summer that he first captured Indians visiting the island of Saint Croix. They had been there to harvest trees for canoes. Ponce de León followed them back to their home island, which set the stage for Spanish dominion. Later, a royal plantation was established on Saint Croix.

Soon after they settled into a house similar to their large home at Salvaleon, Diego acted to dull Ponce de León's influence. He named Juan Ceron to the position of chief justice, which at the time was a similar office to that of governor. By November 4, Ceron had replaced Ponce de León as governor, and the explorer did not argue. None of the people involved knew yet that King Ferdinand had officially acted back in August.

Ponce de León's Justice

It took until the spring of 1510 for things to settle. Two documents—one signed by King Ferdinand and one by Queen Juana—proclaimed that Ponce de León was captain, governor, and judge of the island in question. Ponce de León, now emboldened, felt secure in his position when the documents arrived that June. With Sotomayor urging him on, Ponce de León swiftly arrested Ceron; Miguel Diaz, the chief constable; and Diego de Morales, the deputy. All three men were returned to Spain in July. In appreciation for the support, Sotomayor was appointed chief constable and given a parcel of land that included the Taino village of Guanica. Once Sotomayor saw its poor conditions, however, he had the village relocated to El Aguada.

Ponce de León was named captain of the sea and land, and chief justice of the island by the monarchs. This was an attempt to seal the explorer's control over the island despite it being part of the Columbus family claim as well as to avoid future conflicts in leadership. The king was interested in the promise of San Juan Bautista, and he was careful in his correspondence to treat Ponce de León fairly without inflaming Diego. After all, as in Higüey, Ponce de León had proven himself an able administrator. He managed a successful relationship with the natives while helping to establish a Castilian presence. His men liked and respected him, and, unlike others in the region, his successes far outnumbered his missteps.

Although Castile wanted gold to fatten its royal coffer, the metal meant little to the Tainos. They were more than happy to work alongside the Spaniards in exchange for the superior protection they offered from the cannibalistic Carib Indians, some of whom had settled on San Juan Bautista. However, Guaybana had died in 1510 and was replaced by his brother, who took his name. The new Guaybana, unfortunately for Ponce de León, treated the Spaniards less than favorably.

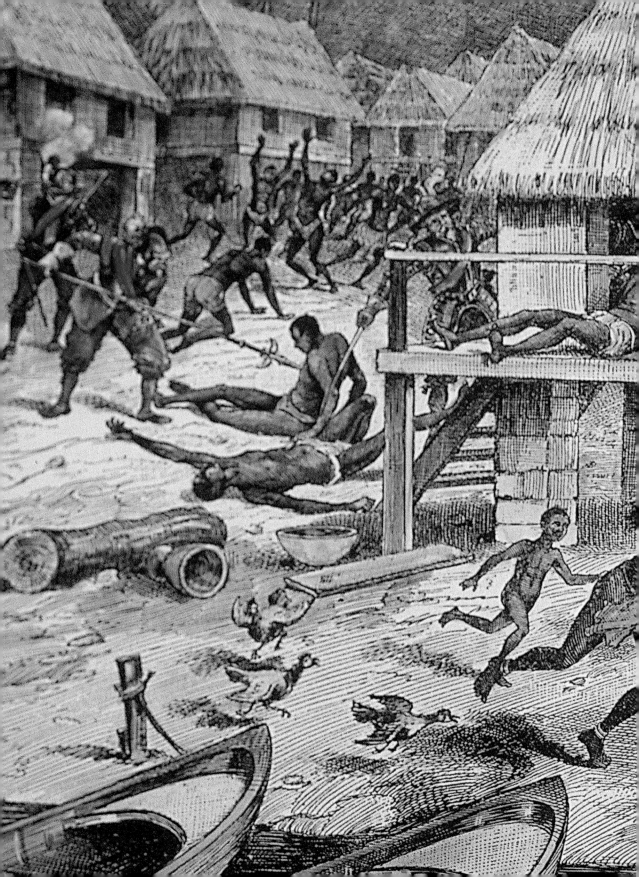

Rebellion

With success came growth. Ponce de León could not possibly control his entire span of territory, or watch every man at every moment. European arrogance, like the attitudes of Sotomayor and his nephew Diego, led to eventual abuse of the Taino Indians. Although the conquistadors attempted to protect them from the Caribs, the attacks continued. This pent-up frustration finally turned into a full rebellion by 1511. According to the historian Don Salvador Brau, as cited in the book *Juan Ponce de León and the Spanish Discovery of Puerto Rico and Florida* by Robert H. Fuson, Guaybana awarded his sister to Sotomayor. She warned him of the coming attack. Despite the advance notice, both perished before Ponce de León and forty other conquistadors could control the attack.

Guaybana was shot and killed as a result of the uprising. His passing so dispirited the Taino Indians that the rebellion ended. Afterward, the entire tribe seemed to have resigned themselves to their new fate: The Spanish had completely taken over their lands and killed nearly their entire population.

The Spanish expected the Taino people to give them gold and food and accept instruction in Christianity. But the Spanish abused the native people, and European diseases, to which the Spaniards were largely immune, began to devastate the Indian population. In 1511 they rebelled but had little success against the better-armed Spanish, who again conquered them.

As the year progressed, European governments and boundaries finally began to take shape. The Council of Castilla proclaimed on May 14 that Diego Columbus's claims were indeed valid and all the Columbus family holdings, including the island of San Juan Bautista, legally belonged to him. Ponce de León learned of this in a letter from King Ferdinand.

Juan Ceron also shipped gold back to King Ferdinand that month, which resulted in another return letter from the Spanish Crown. This letter considered the idea of Ponce de León seeking new lands.

Early December saw Ceron positioned as the island's governor, although Ponce de León remained its military leader. The island hoisted a flag bearing a coat of arms that day, the first of its kind in the New World.

That year, 1512, continued much as the prior year had. Although Diego kept applying pressure to Ponce de León, neither man was happy with their relationship. Finally, after a suggestion from the king, the problems between them would finally be solved once and for all.

6
LAND OF FLOWERS AND FEAR

Whereas you, Ponce de León, have requested that I grant you the authority to go to discover and settle the islands of Benimy [sic], under certain condition, in order to bestow my favor upon you I grant you the authority to discover and settle the said Island, with the provision that it is not one of those that has already been discovered.
—King Ferdinand's contract with Ponce de León, 1512

In the summer of 1511, the royal treasurer, Miguel de Pasamonte, shared a secret with Ponce de León: He said that there was vast unexplored land to the northwest that was populated with potential slaves. Dating back to at least 1508, several vessels had sailed this region and brought back such reports. Since the Spanish Crown had not yet authorized any true expedition of the area, the exact nature of the land and its inhabitants was unknown.

The Fountain of Youth

The result of this news was that the king also alerted Ponce de León about information concerning a natural spring or fountain in those lands, a story that was mentioned in one way or another over time by the Taino Indians. When King Ferdinand began discussing this mission with Ponce de León, he made the request that he search for the Fountain of Bimini.

The whole notion of the Fountain of Youth can be found in one historic text after another, and widespread legends place it everywhere around the world. Given the frequent references to such a fountain by the region's natives, there's little doubt that such stories made their way back to Castile.

Today, many people think that Ponce de León was a mad explorer seeking the Fountain of Youth for himself, but he was actually searching on behalf of his king. By the time of the expedition, Ferdinand, at sixty years of age, had married Germaine de Foix, thirty-five years younger than himself. He had most likely hoped that such mysterious waters existed to increase their time together.

The modern city of St. Augustine, Florida, is near the site where Ponce de León and his Spanish conquistadors first landed in search of the Fountain of Youth. They came ashore in what is now the continental United States in 1513.

New Expeditions

Unlike their collective interest in what we now know was merely legendary, both King Ferdinand and Ponce de León also sought treasure in the form of gold. They were wealthy men, but neither stopped at any opportunity to gain riches. Ponce de León, however, at about thirty-eight years of age, embraced the idea of establishing new colonies and bringing his farming and administration methods to new lands.

And because the possession of the new territory was uncontested, the king was more than happy to grant it to Ponce de León and not to Columbus's family. By this time, Ponce de León, already formally the governor of San Juan Bautista, realized that the problems with Diego Columbus were far from settled. On August 1, King Ferdinand directed Miguel de Pasamonte to begin discussing new voyages of discovery with Ponce de León.

However, at the very same time, Christopher Columbus's brother Bartolomeo made a proposal to the Crown for the same region. Despite it being a superior offer, Diego's political actions influenced the king to instead grant the commission to Ponce de León. The king was indeed fond of Ponce de León and of his loyalty to his kingdom. The decision resulted in a formal contract between Ponce de León and Castile in March 1512. It contained financial obligations, a time limit, and other constraints, but it was clearly written to allow Ponce de León undisputed claim of any land he found. By this time, though, he was no longer governor, and Diego's handpicked men began to use the government against him, delaying any future voyage.

In January 1512, before the contract could be signed, Francisco de Lizaur took possession of Ponce de León's financial records from his time as governor. This allowed Lizaur to question everything he had done, harass him, and spread misinformation about the way he had handled the island's affairs.

Diego's followers confiscated Ponce de León's ship, and a friend of his, Juan Bono de Quejo, was jailed. As a result of Lizaur's actions, Ponce de León was effectively a prisoner on his own island while still negotiating with Castile for his next expedition.

Pasamonte, also a friend and admirer of Ponce de León, investigated the claims coming from Diego, which resulted in Lizaur being arrested and returned to Europe that May. The king, tired of Diego's tricks (although there is no evidence that Diego himself directed or knew of Lizaur's actions), appointed Rodrigo de Moscoso as the island's new governor, replacing Ceron, who was in Castile at the time.

Ceron was ordered to return Ponce de León's ship that August and free de Quejo, who remained in jail. The order included an invitation for Ponce de León to come to Castile for a royal audience, but he turned it down, preferring to get back to mounting his new expedition.

The year ended with Ponce de León being named warden of the fortress nearing completion at Caparra. He also returned to his role as treasurer, and gained responsibility for the royal lands and disbursement of the Taino population. As the New Year began, de Quejo captained the *Santa Maria de la Consolacion* from Spain into port carrying with it the new governor, Rodrigo de Moscoso.

Things had settled down enough for Ponce de León to feel confident to embark on his new mission. His first stop was Santo Domingo, where he was required to post a bond for his voyage that January.

The second stop was at Salvaleon, Ponce de León's estate. He collected supplies of food and freshwater. Ponce de León also selected several of his crew members there, too, because records show that two of the three expedition ships were registered in Salvaleon's port of Yuma. These were the *Santiago*, registered January 29, and the *Santa Maria de la Consolacion*, registered February 5. Along with the *San Cristobal*, an estimated sixty-five people joined Ponce de León on his voyage to Bimini. One woman, Juana Ruiz, who boarded at Yuma, was among that crew. She became the first European female to set foot on North America's mainland.

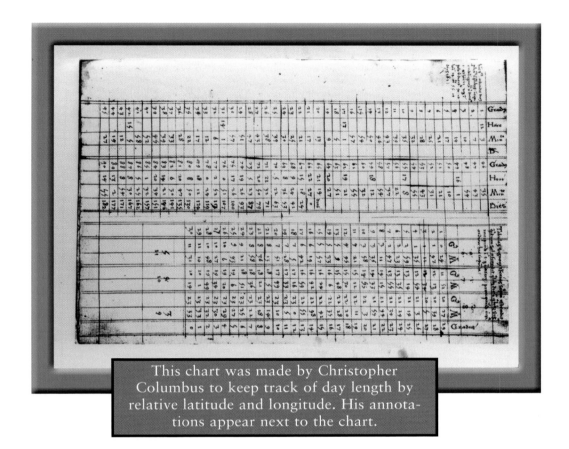

This chart was made by Christopher Columbus to keep track of day length by relative latitude and longitude. His annotations appear next to the chart.

Locating Bimini Island

At this time, Europeans still imagined that only Africa and the Atlantic Ocean separated Europe from Asia. Sixteenth-century maps show vast expanses of water and several of the larger islands that had been recently discovered, such as Cuba and Jamaica, but Bimini's placement on period maps often changed.

This sixteenth-century map of Florida and Cuba was drawn by Theodor de Bry for a series about great voyages of the time. The map is inaccurate; Cuba is too large, and the long peninsula of Florida is somewhat stunted.

As research continued, however, the location of Bimini and the Florida coast were confused into one island. According to analysis from Columbus's own logs, he had three different opportunities to sail toward, and discover, Florida, but each time he headed farther south.

The three ships set sail on March 12. Antonio de Herrera y Tordesillas wrote the only official account of the expedition nearly a century later for King Felipe II of Castile who had made him an official historian in 1596. Herrera, now considered a good plagiarist and bad historian, stole from his predecessors, but it is his work that has survived. His report is most likely a composite of what actually happened. For Ponce de León's mission, Herrera seems to have taken most of his material from Alonso de Chaves, who wrote his works in 1537.

On April 11, they spotted land and dubbed it Tierra La Florida (Land of Flowers), honoring its lush beauty as well as Easter Sunday (Pascua de Flores), the day of their discovery. From the records, it was most likely Abaco Island that they saw before they spotted what is now known as the state of Florida. By April 28, as they scouted the eastern shoreline, the ships encountered what was later called the Gulf Stream, perhaps as important a discovery as the land itself. After all, knowledge of the Gulf Stream forever altered how people navigated the surrounding waters. Knowledge of the Gulf Stream, or the Bahama Channel, provided a new sea route from the West Indies to Spain. While Columbus discovered the trade winds that helped his ships swiftly move from east to west, the Gulf Stream proved to be the best way back to Europe. Once Ponce de León and his crew charted and understood the swift-running waters of the Gulf Stream, it became apparent why ports such as Cuba were so important. It also helped determine the location for St. Augustine, the oldest European settlement on the American mainland.

Unfriendly Encounters

Once on land, the first Indian encounter showed that, unlike the Taino, these natives would not be as welcoming. Capturing a member of the Ais tribe after a skirmish, the explorers learned that the land was known as Cautio. By the end of the month, Ponce de León's crew neared Sanibel Island and encountered another local tribe called the Caloosa, who also reacted hostilely toward the men. Chaves wrote that the Indians, led by the cacique, Carlos, attacked the men and wounded two of them. Ponce de León was forced to fight back in order to protect his crew. Finally, the vessels sailed to Estero Island for repairs.

Ponce de León and the three ships went as far north as the area now known as Jacksonville and also surveyed what he named the Martyrs, which we now call the Florida Keys, before turning west. Later, near the contemporary city of Jupiter, they encountered a tribe numbered at sixty men and somehow captured one to act as their guide. They named this area Rio de la Cruz. For several weeks, the ships sailed up and down the western coast of Florida, studying its many inlets, capes, and bays, naming each as they continued.

By mid-June, Ponce de León again encountered a hostile tribe, which laid a trap for his ships. The Indians attacked, but their spears and arrows did not travel far enough to reach the ships' decks. Meanwhile, the European artillery kept them at bay.

Ponce de León's Return to Spain

By the end of June, Ponce de León decided to return home. It was a leisurely trip, with many stops along the way to study new, smaller islands. Some of these were named the Tortugas. Now called the Dry Tortugas and part of the Florida Keys, they today claim the oldest location name in the United States other than Florida.

Documented history indicates that Ponce de León attempted to find out if the natives knew that their homeland was not an island as he had previously believed, but part of America. As he named provinces, implying that it was larger than an island, he still had trouble believing it. Indeed, Ponce de León had set foot on mainland America without immediately realizing it.

For long voyages, European explorers of the fifteenth, sixteenth, and seventeenth centuries often used caravels, which were light sailing ships. The typical caravel weighed fifty to sixty tons and was about seventy-five feet long, with two to four pole masts, and lateen-rigged (triangular) sails. The Portuguese developed caravels for exploring the coast of Africa.

By early August, Ponce de León and his crew left Florida behind to seek Bimini itself, now that it was apparent that they were separate landmasses. In July, they had happened upon on old Indian woman at an island stop and brought her aboard ship. She told them the island they found was called Bahama, known today as Grand Bahama. Around this time, they also encountered a ship led by Diego Miruelo, who had been sent by Diego Columbus to ensure the safety of Ponce de León's expedition.

Miruelo and his small craft joined the expedition, leisurely sailing toward San Juan Bautista. But as hurricane season got underway, the seas became dangerous, and the small ship was lost. Luckily, however, the captain and his crew were rescued by some of Ponce de León's men. In all, Ponce de León and his crew sailed for 230 days, seeing sights and meeting people never before encountered by Europeans.

Diego Columbus's Rise to Power

On June 11, Diego Columbus brought a group of followers with him to San Juan Bautista, and they were all appointed to government positions on the island. Unlike his father, Diego reveled in the trappings of high society. He had married the duke of Alva's daughter and handpicked the cavaliers and bluebloods who were to accompany him to the New World. Although highly educated, his appointees were an arrogant bunch, whose mistreatment of the natives would eventually lead to great trouble.

As if to welcome Ponce de León on that same day, the dreaded Carib Indians burned down the settlement at Caparra. Ponce de León's wife and children escaped the burning flames that resulted from the attack of hundreds of maddened Indians.

Diego, always seeking a political angle, blamed Ponce de León's poor judgment for the attack, claiming that he established Caparra in a vulnerable location. Diego then dispatched Juan Enriquez to seek revenge. The attacking Indians were never found, leading Ponce de León, upon his return, to conclude that they were from a neighboring island. The damage, though, was done, and Caparra lay in cinders. Moreover, Diego exerted further Castilian influence over the entire region of islands, to the detriment of the more peaceful Taino tribes.

Ponce de León surveyed the situation on San Juan Bautista and saw that Diego was prepared to use anything to discredit him. He knew he had to act carefully, balancing his desire for revenge against the Caribs and Diego Columbus.

Ponce de León Goes Before the Royal Court

Finally, Ponce de León decided that enough was enough. He made plans to return to Castile to have his overdue visit to the court of King Ferdinand. Aboard the *San Cristobal*, captained by Juan Perez de Ortubia, he left the Caribbean region in April 1514. In less than a month he was returning to his homeland for the first time in over a decade.

Ponce de León brought with him his knowledge of the area, which he shared in detail with Juan Diaz de Solis, pilot-major of the Casa de Contratacíon—the house of the official maps and records of all Castilian maritime exploits. These records were collectively known as the *padron real*. It was at this time that officials recorded details from Ponce de León's trip to "Bimini" and the "discovery" of Florida. Just weeks earlier, Vasco Nuñez de Balboa's trip to the South Seas, known today as the Pacific Ocean, had first been entered into the record books. It was a great time for exploration, and the Castilians were well in the forefront of such efforts.

The records are somewhat hazy, however, as to when Ponce de León met with King Ferdinand in Valladolid. It could have been before or after his September visit to the Casa de Contratacíon. Regardless, the king was delighted to see a man he admired. A gift of 5,000 pesos worth of gold was welcomed, and the king finally had a chance to hear from the New World's leading authority.

Don Juan Ponce de León

While visiting the king, Ponce de León was knighted and given a personal coat of arms, a sign of great stature. He was the first of the conquistadors to receive such an honor, and he certainly deserved the award given his accomplishments on behalf of the Crown. In

Castilian society, being knighted meant he would be addressed as Don, similar to the British use of "Sir." His San Juan Bautista titles were reinforced as well, so he remained captain-general of the island for life, perpetual member of the city council, and chief justice. Additionally, he was given jurisdiction over the Windward Islands. The king reimbursed his expenses, and Ponce de León was also given a set salary of 50,000 maravedis a year.

By October 4, Ponce de León received several declarations (documents) to transport, including one naming Balboa governor of the South Sea. More important to Ponce de León were the agreements signed by King Ferdinand regarding entitlements to Florida and Bimini, including naming Ponce de León the area's governor. Not forgetting the Carib attack, Ponce de León was also named captain of the Armada and charged with subduing the Carib Indians, although that usually meant exterminating them outright.

With the goal of settling Bimini and Florida, Ponce de León could begin afresh; clear of any entanglements with Diego Columbus and his political cronies. He was given a three-year charter (contract) to do so, using his own financial resources to accomplish the task. The key difference was its clause that called for an attack against the Caribs. It also specifically commanded that Diego lend assistance to Ponce de León's efforts.

After the native people of the New World welcomed the Spanish and shared their knowledge, the Spaniards repaid the favor by forcing the Indians to bow to European supremacy, making them convert to Christianity, or enslaving them.

The Requirement

An interesting new clause in the charter outlined the fate of the Indians. Since Columbus had first brought Indians to Europe, a great debate had occurred about what to do with them. Most Europeans favored using them as slaves, although Queen Isabella seemed to have some trouble with the notion. None of this stopped slaves from entering the Caribbean region from Africa, however, which led to centuries of buying and selling African men and women.

The Requirement was a legal document. It was a legal agreement that was read by the conquistador to the Indians and then physically shown to them. This act satisfied any qualms the Crown had regarding what happened next to the Native Americans. The Requirement meant that the Indians had to acknowledge the European sovereignty (supremacy) of their islands in the name of God. If they agreed to the Requirement, they would remain free to stay with their land and families. And while not required to convert to Catholicism, it was to be offered at every opportunity. Any Indian ignoring this directive would be subject to European justice in the form of enslavement or death.

The Spanish were among the most committed Europeans when it came to spreading their religious views. By the sixteenth century, Catholicism was rapidly growing across the continent, and several countries devoted much effort to missionary work. With the Spanish exerting great influence in the New World, they had hoped to bring their own religious truth to the natives to save their souls. After spending eight centuries ridding their lands of Moors, the Christians were feeling righteous and proud.

Many European explorers read the Requirement to the natives, who did little more than stare in bewilderment at the sounds coming from the explorers mouths. While it might have made sense to those at court, it certainly didn't have the desired effect in the New World.

Understanding the Indians

The Casa de Contratacíon's staff knew that Ponce de León—now the captain of the Armada and governor of the area—would need firepower to handle the Caribs, and set about preparing a fleet. The problem was that the operation was so impoverished that it could not have new ships built. Around mid-September, however, while the official proclamations were being drafted, the Casa purchased three used ships and spent six months refurbishing them. Ponce de León's fleet of three caravels included the *Barbola*, the *Santa Maria*, and the *Santiago*.

Ponce de León was less certain about the need for such a fleet. If one were necessary, it was not to punish the Carib Indians but instead to police the seas. His intention was to prevent his fellow countrymen from enslaving the more peaceful Indians.

Near the end of May 1515, Ponce de León was prepared to leave Europe behind forever. The fleet's first stop was Guadeloupe, a known Carib stronghold. Surviving historical records agree that sailors collecting freshwater there were set upon by Indians. Instead of facing the conflict, the Spanish fleet escaped. They were not ready for such a fight.

Ponce de León returned to San Juan Bautista in late July. Now that he was back in familiar territory, he named Captain Inigo de Zuniga as his fleet commander and sent the ships to the Lesser Antilles.

European conquests in the New World decimated the Taino. Through enslavement and disease, the Indian population, which numbered more than one million before the Spanish conquest, was reduced to fewer than 4,000 people.

Although Ponce de León could make a distinction between the savage Carib Indians and the more peaceful Tainos, his fellow countrymen were less discriminating. As a result, virtually the entire Taino population was enslaved and their lives turned to misery. Complicating things was the administration of the island's current governor, Sancho Velazquez, who arrived at the end of November 1514. Velazquez viewed Ponce de León as his political rival, a competition that slowed progress for all. It probably thrilled Ponce de León when Velazquez was finally imprisoned in 1519 by his successor, Antonio de la Gama, Ponce de León's son-in-law.

By this time, there were so few Tainos left that growing demands for slave labor led to a brisk slave trade with ships bringing Africans to the New World. It is believed that the new slaves fell victim to the deadly health threat of both small-pox and measles. In 1519, there was an epidemic that left many Tainos and Africans dead because they had no immunity against the deadly European diseases.

Protecting His Claims

Ponce de León's efforts to secure Bimini and Florida were nearly derailed when, six months after leaving Europe in February 1516, King Ferdinand died. Politics complicated matters as Ferdinand's grandson Carlos was named king in his place. But Carlos could not assume the throne immediately, for he was already king of the Netherlands. Following the late King Ferdinand's instructions, a regency was established that left Castile's government under the control of Cardinal Francisco Ximenez de Cisneros, and Aragon under the administration of Archbishop Alonso of Zaragosa.

Ponce de León arrived again in Europe in November 1516 and stayed until 1518 to assure everything he was involved in would remain unaffected. He needn't have worried; Ponce de León was a well-respected servant to the Crown, seen as successful as both a farmer and an administrator. There would be little benefit in removing him from authority.

Another potential reason for Ponce de León's return was to ensure that his three-boat fleet was dismantled. This order was issued on December 4, 1516, but not carried out until four months later. The liquidation of the fleet was completed exactly a year later, with Ponce de León in the background ensuring its completion.

Ponce de León's activities in Castile during this time are not well documented. It is known, however, that he was at court when word arrived of two unauthorized visits to his new territory. The first occurred in April 1517, when his former pilot, Anton de Alaminos, was aboard one of three vessels destined for the Yucatán Peninsula. The trip, which was the first expedition to the peninsula and one of the first extensive meetings with the Maya (Columbus had encountered Mayan Indians in the Gulf of Honduras during his final voyage of discovery in 1502), was a disaster, and the three ships limped toward home.

Alaminos felt the best way to return to Cuba was to sail around Florida. The others agreed and let him lead the way. Alaminos guided the ships to the exact spot they had used four years earlier. Then the Caloosa Indians threatened them, making the crew ever more watchful as they restocked their water. Sure enough, the Caloosas attacked. Six men, including Alaminos, were wounded. They escaped, but not without fighting and more death. At one point the flagship ran aground in the Florida Keys, but the fleet managed its way back to Havana, Cuba.

In the summer of 1517, word reached Cardinal Cisneros that the governor of Cuba, Diego de Valazquez, had taken a party to the Florida Keys, enslaving 300 Matacumbes Indians. Cisneros issued a royal *cedula*, a form of proclamation that criticized Valazquez for encroaching on territory clearly marked as Don Juan Ponce de León's.

Returning to the New World

By April 1518, Ponce de León was satisfied. He was free to return to the New World, which he now thought of as his home. His family had remained there while he worked to make sure his titles and holdings were secure.

Returning to San Juan Bautista in May, Ponce de León was surprised to learn that the island was about to be renamed Puerto Rico. Those who survived the burning of the Caparra settlement were eager to rebuild on the landmass set in the harbor, where Old San Juan is today. At first they called their new home el Puerto Rico de San Juan—the Rich Port of San Juan—and in a short time, the town became San Juan and the island Puerto Rico.

To Ponce de León the notion was absurd. A farmer by trade, he cited the poor land and difficulties presented while trying to raise families, livestock, and crops on such a small space. The majority of the people, though, believed otherwise. They preferred the notion of harbor trade, letting commerce dominate over agriculture. A vote taken in 1521 sealed the settlement's future, and Ponce de León gracefully accepted the official decision.

Ponce de León spent much of 1518 reacquainting himself with his family, his holdings, and the changes in and around the Caribbean. However, Florida loomed large in his mind because his charter, though extended during his European visit, now had a fast approaching deadline.

7

A CAREER IN TWILIGHT

Among my services, I discovered at my own expense, the island of Florida and others in its district. I intend to explore the coast of the said island further, and see whether it is an island, or whether it connects with [Cuba], or any other, and I shall endeavor to learn all I can. I shall set out to pursue my voyage hence in five or six days.
—Letter from Ponce de León to King Charles V, 1521

The new year brought bad news. Ponce de León's close friend Balboa had died in Panama. Not only were they friends, but they had been named governor on the same day. Ponce de León recognized that he was aging. This notion was further realized when his wife, Leónor, died during the second half of the year.

This 1588 map is a fairly accurate representation of what is now the southeastern United States. Florida prospered under Spanish rule until the eighteenth century, when the English moved to control the eastern seaboard, while the Spanish focused their attention on Latin and South America. In 1526, Spanish explorer Panfilo de Narváez, who arrived from Spain with 600 men and 5 ships, was given permission to conquer the land of Florida by Emperor Charles V. Narváez died before he could do so.

'RIO.

79

40

Cum Priuilegio.

anara
ay.

Guax
uli.

Xuala.

Xuaquile

Chalaqua

Rio Canaas

Rio Iordan

Antiunes

P. S. Helena Flu.

P. S. Helena

Cafaqui

Catilachegue.

Aymay.

Rio Sero

si

Rio de Nieues

P. de S.
Maria.

Baya baxa

Baya de S. Ioſeph.

Baya de
Baxos

Baya de Spo
Santo.

Iuan de
Ponte.

C. de
Cruz.

C. Grueſo.

ORIENS

Canal de Bahama

Rio de
Cori
ento.

C. de Cañareal

Iucayonoqz.

30

Bahama

Aboa

Rio de
Aguada.

La Florida.

Binini

FLORIDA
Hieron. Chiaues.

Rio de
Canoas

Martyres

de Tortugas

Cancri

79

It should be noted that while Ponce de León was shuttling between Europe and the Caribbean, other explorers were setting out farther west. Hernán Cortés was determined to colonize Mexico, and Alonsó Alvarez Pineda was exploring the Gulf of Mexico for the purposes of colonization. What makes these voyages interesting is that, in most cases, they surveyed portions of the western Florida coastline and began adding details to the maps. Most began including Tierra La Florida, with Pineda's map crediting Ponce de León for its discovery. All these explorations involved their own version of politics, betrayal, and secrets kept from one another and especially Ponce de León, as people drew near his New World holdings.

Time Grows Short

By 1520, it became evident that Ponce de León either had to mount his second expedition or lose land to another explorer. Already word had come back that Diego Miruelo had mapped the Pensacola Bay, while others had been violating Ponce de León's contracts by raiding the land, and capturing Indians for the slave trade. Vasquez de Ayollon also sailed farther north in 1520, managing to map the Carolina coast, which was then claimed by Spain.

Ponce de León spent most of the year working out the arrangements and outfitting his ships for the journey.

While he used some 6,000 pesos, he still required financial assistance, which came from close friend Pedro de la Mata. De la Mata joined Ponce de León on this second voyage, but first the men went to Santo Domingo to finalize some of the planning. By February, both men were back in Puerto Rico.

For some reason, neither Ponce de León nor his contemporaries carefully chronicled this voyage, so most historians today rely on Henry Harrisse's nineteenth-century report. Harrisse gathered his documents from various sources, including two surviving letters written by Ponce de León himself.

In one of these letters, dated February 19, 1521, to Cardinal Adrian of Tortosa (who would become Pope Adrian VI just a year later), Ponce de León explained his present circumstances. He identified that his three daughters were married, which he felt freed him to pursue his new mission. Ponce de León also wrote that he would be leaving five or six days after writing the letter and taking two ships with him.

The second letter was to King Charles V, also known as Carlos, who was then the ruler of the Holy Roman Empire. In it, Ponce de León clearly stated that he hoped to determine if Florida was a very large island or actually a larger landmass. What he never realized was that Pineda's explorations a year or so earlier had already settled the issue.

87

Ponce de León probably encountered the hostile Caloosa Indians in mid-March, and historians believe that he died from injuries inflicted in a battle with them. Scientific evidence suggests that the Caloosa Indians occupied the west coast of Florida for thousands of years until they disappeared without a trace in the 1700s.

An Untimely Death

Ponce de León's two ships left Puerto Rico in late February 1521, loaded with approximately a hundred men, ten horses, and other assorted animals designed to start a colony. He traveled to the Gulf Coast, recognizing that his fellow explorers were finding wondrous lands with alarming regularity. There was some pressure on him, mostly self-induced, to do something or be eclipsed by his colleagues.

Ponce de León most likely arrived at Florida in mid-March, near where he first encountered the hostile Caloosa Indians. No records have survived to indicate exactly where he set down and began to settle the area. His previous actions indicated a preference for farmland on the mainland and near readily accessible water, which he needed for both drinking and irrigation.

There is also a record of a confrontation with Indians by early that July that led to a battle. These may have been the Caloosa Indians, which would place the colony south of present-day Tampa Bay.

Even the reason for the conflict is not known. What has survived is information that Ponce de León's nephew Hernán was killed during the attack and buried at sea. Ponce de León himself was shot in his leg with a reed arrow and severely wounded, forcing the Spanish settlers to abandon the land and set sail.

For Ponce de León's wound to be so grave, historians have long speculated that the arrows were poison-tipped, but this information has not been proven. Given how long he survived after being wounded, it's more likely he died from a routine infection. The inadequacy of medical knowledge at the time makes this entirely possible.

Ponce de León's ship made it safely to Havana, Cuba, while the other sailed to Vera Cruz, Mexico, arriving around July 24. There, the men reported the event to Cortés.

A fatally wounded Ponce de Leon is carried back to his ship for the voyage to Cuba. Some historians believe that he was shot with a poison-tipped arrow. He eventually died from his wounds.

Ponce de León was, if anything, a practical man. Sensing his approaching death, he most likely directed what was to become of his holdings, attempting to protect his family's future. He wished for the holdings to be sold for cash, which was to be used to purchase livestock that would again be sold at a greater value. This final sum of money would be directed to his surviving family. Records indicate, however, that his chosen executors instead kept the cash for themselves.

In Cuba, Ponce de León died from his wounds at forty-seven years of age.

8

FLORIDA TODAY

In this sepulcher rest the bones of a man who was a lion by name and still more by nature.

—Translation of Latin inscription on
Ponce de León's tomb in Cuba

Ponce de León's passing did not merit much attention at the time, with the focus of exploration and discovery having by then shifted to areas in Mexico and South America. Despite his solid reputation in the New World and in Spain, Ponce de León's passing was a quiet event. He lived his life not seeking attention and so too in death, he went quietly. There is even information recorded about what became of his family. In 1559, his remains were taken from Havana, Cuba, a location that was alien to him, to San Juan Cathedral in Puerto Rico, where they remain to this day. His epitaph reads:

In the Name of God
Under the pontificate of his holiness Pius X and occupying the Episcopal seat of Puerto Rico Monsignor Guillermo Jones. Moved to this Cathedral Church, from the convent of Santo Tomas de Aquino where they had been interred since 1559, the mortal remains of

JUAN PONCE DE LEÓN

A native of Terria de Campos whose gallant deeds were evidence of his noble and pure lineage. Soldier in Granada, Captain in Española, conqueror and Governor of San Juan del Borinquen. Discoverer and first Governor of Florida; valiant military man; skillful leader, loyal subject. Honest administrator, loving father and industrious and consistent colonist. He surrendered his soul to God and his body to the Earth in Havana (June 1521). To his venerable memory and in honor of the Christian civilization introduced through his impetus, founded by his bravery, and spread by his diligent cooperation in this bountiful Puerto Rican land, a devote tribute is consecrated.

The Spanish Club of San Juan
AD 1909

Finally, in 1882, a statue was erected of Ponce de León in the Plaza of San Jose. It was cast from a brass cannon abandoned by the British in 1797.

People mill about in the streets of St. Augustine, Florida, one of the oldest cities in the United States. It has a rich history. In 1513, Ponce de Leon came ashore in the vicinity of St. Augustine and claimed the entire continent for Spain. In 1565, Pedro Menendez de Aviles was commissioned by the king of Spain to dispatch the neighboring French settlers. Menendez established St. Augustine, then marched forty miles with 500 men in a hurricane to surprise the French. In 1586, Sir Francis Drake, returning from his trip around the world, stumbled across St. Augustine and burned it down. The struggling colonists rebuilt their city.

Florida was finally completely settled in 1528, under the watchful discretion of Panfilo de Narváez, an explorer who had left Spain with 600 men and 5 ships—more than enough to give any attacking Indians pause. When Pedro Menendez de Aviles established the settlement at what is now St. Augustine, Florida was well on its way to becoming a major part of the Spanish Empire.

Florida continued to prosper under Spanish rule well into the eighteenth century. At that point, the British controlled the rest of the eastern coast and the Spanish concentrated their attention and resources farther south in both Latin and South America.

During the Seven Years' War (1756–1763) with Spain, the British captured Cuba and exchanged it for Florida in 1763. The region was split in two, with both halves remaining loyal to the British Crown during the American Revolution. One region was lost to Spain in 1781, as Spain aided France in its war against Britain, while the other region was governed under Spanish control in 1784.

Vying for Power and Territory

The Spanish were surprised by the number of new Americans streaming in to colonize the region. They ceded control of the land to the United States in 1821 (300 years after Ponce de León's second voyage) under the terms of the Adams-Onis Treaty.

Florida's official statehood was granted on March 3, 1845.

Puerto Rico was a much-desired location for European expansion and, in the years following Ponce de León's death, the Spanish had to repel a French incursion. They briefly lost control of the island in 1598 to the British but regained it after the plague decimated the British army. The English once again tried to retake the island during the same war that led Spain to regain Florida in 1781. By 1809, Napoléon was controlling Spain. He allowed a certain degree of self-governance and the people elected their first representative to the mother country.

By 1815, the gold supply on the island was exhausted, so the economy revolved around shipping and agriculture with sugarcane as its leading crop. A movement grew for Puerto Rican independence, with protests and rebellions occurring on a regular basis. The Castilian Crown finally abolished slavery in 1873, decades after Europe had almost uniformly done the same. Finally, in 1897, the Autonomic Charter was established, granting the island self-governance but not outright freedom. As a result of the Spanish-American War one year later, however, Spain gave Puerto Rico to the United States as a territory. To this day, there remain factions that desire complete freedom for the island while others would like it to become the fifty-first state of the United States.

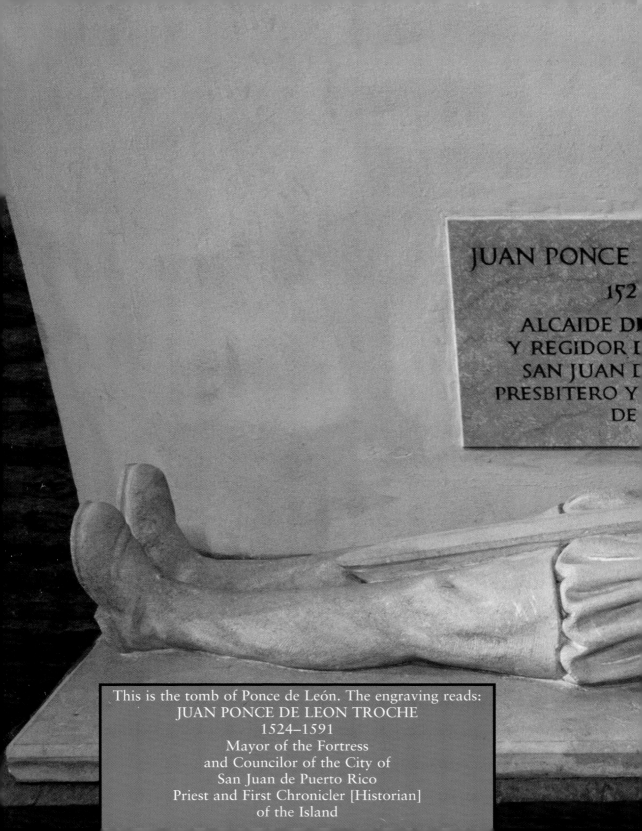

JUAN PONCE

152

ALCAIDE D

Y REGIDOR D

SAN JUAN D

PRESBITERO Y

DE

This is the tomb of Ponce de León. The engraving reads:
JUAN PONCE DE LEON TROCHE
1524–1591
Mayor of the Fortress
and Councilor of the City of
San Juan de Puerto Rico
Priest and First Chronicler [Historian]
of the Island

E LEON TROCHE
— 1591

LA FORTALEZA
LA CIUDAD DE
PUERTO RICO,
RIMER CRONISTA
A ISLA.

Remembering Ponce de León

Here and there, modern visitors to Puerto Rico will find a plaza or street named after the unique explorer, but nothing grand. As Ponce de León did not seek personal fame, his memory is a humble one, sadly united with the myth of the Fountain of Youth and little else. His style of exploration, his considerate dealings with the natives, and his attention to detail won him great admiration in the court of King Ferdinand, but those accomplishments are now sadly faded.

His white house in Old San Juan stands in ruins, a minor stop on any walking tour of the island. Perhaps the largest recognition of Juan Ponce de León's influence is the naming of Puerto Rico's second largest province, Ponce. Founded in 1670, it is one of the largest cities in the Caribbean.

The Spanish culture and heritage remain strongly alive in both regions, blended over the centuries with that of the native Indians and two hundred years of American development.

With the success of the settlement at St. Augustine, Pedro Menendez de Aviles has received almost as much attention in Florida as Ponce de León himself did. In fact, visitors to the area might be confused, thinking Ponce de León discovered the land as well as established the settlement, when in truth he only landed north of there. Still, St. Augustine has adopted Ponce de León and named many locations after him. There is even a Fountain of Youth attraction, perpetuating the misconception about Ponce de León, especially since he was never told where to look for the fabled waters.

Navigators today still use the Gulf Stream to plot their courses, rarely acknowledging Ponce de León's discovery. Similarly, his habit of landing where fresh water was plentiful and the land fertile was followed by dozens of explorers who followed in his footsteps.

In an era when new discoveries were made with amazing regularity, Ponce de León's accomplishments were appreciated, but his true gift was his style of management and his loyalty to the Crown. He set a standard of excellence that few of his contemporaries were able to match. It is these qualities that should allow Ponce de León to remain one of the best-recognized explorers in history.

CHRONOLOGY

1460 or 1474   Birth of Juan Ponce de León.

1493   Ponce de León accompanies Christopher Columbus on his second voyage to the New World.

1502   Ponce de León visits the New World for a second time.

1504   Proving himself a natural diplomat, Ponce de León settles a Taino uprising.

1506   Although his mission is a secret one, Ponce de León first visits San Juan Bautista.

1508   Ponce de León is involved in the conquest of Cuba. He officially explores San Juan Bautista for the Castilian Crown.

1509 Ponce de León explores Jamaica. He is named governor of San Juan Bautista by King Ferdinand.

1510 Ponce de León is named captain of sea and land and chief justice of the region.

1512 King Ferdinand contracts Ponce de León to explore the island of Bimini.

1513 Vasco Nuñez de Balboa, Ponce de León's friend, crosses the Isthmus of Panama and becomes the first European to see the Pacific Ocean. Ponce de León explores the western coast of Florida.

1514 Ponce de León returns to Europe and is knighted by the Spanish Crown.

1515 Ponce de León returns to San Juan Bautista.

1516 King Ferdinand dies; Ponce de León returns once more to Europe. Diego Miruelo maps Pensacola Bay.

1518 Ponce de León returns to San Juan Bautista.

1519 Alonsó Alvarez Pineda is first to realize that Florida is part of a continent.

1520 Pineda sails across the Gulf of Mexico.

1521 Ponce de León is mortally wounded during an Indian attack and brought back to Cuba, where he dies.

GLOSSARY

adelantado   Indian title for frontier governor.

cacique   Spanish title for tribal chief.

caravel   Common fifteenth-century sailing ship known for its small size and high speed. It was popularized by Portugal's Prince Henry the Navigator.

Carthage   Middle Eastern country that conquered much of Europe. The Carthaginians helped populate what is known today as Spain.

Casa de Contratacíon   Spanish organization charged with the official record keeping for the country's maritime exploits.

cassava bread   A long-lasting bread made from the yucca plant. Cassava bread is a profitable baked good for long voyages made popular by Juan Ponce de León.

Castile   One of the two regions located on the Iberian Peninsula that occupy the land known today as Spain.

cede   To yield or grant by treaty.

Celts   A people who lived in central and western Europe, including the Irish, Welsh, and Scots.

conquistador   A Spanish explorer and conqueror, but not quite a soldier.

encomienda   A land grant, usually dozens, if not hundreds, of acres.

epitaph   An inscription on or at a tomb or grave in memory of the person buried there.

faction   A government party or group.

Granada   A region on the Iberian Peninsula ruled by Moors for many centuries; part of Spain.

Gulf Stream   A strong, fast-moving current found in the Gulf of Mexico; referred to as the Bahama Channel.

hardtack   A flour and water cracker, made in advance of long voyages, but which did not have the same longevity as cassava bread.

Glossary

Holy Roman Empire A territory that included much of Germany, Italy, and Lorraine and Burgundy in France.

incursion A hostile entrance into a territory; raid.

maravedis A measure of Castilian money, less than a peso, in the sixteenth century.

Muslims Followers of Islam and its holy book, the Koran.

padron real Official maritime maps and records maintained in Spain's Casa de Contratacíon.

peso A measure of Spanish money still in use today.

Phoenicians Canaanites based on the Syrian coast and renamed by the Greeks. They migrated throughout the Middle East and Europe.

Reconquest The name given to the 800-year effort to expel from the Iberian region the Moors, or Muslims, whose ancestors came from Africa.

regent One who governs a kingdom in the absence of a sovereign ruler such as a king.

repartimiento The assignment of workers to the owner of an encomienda.

FOR MORE INFORMATION

American Geographical Society
120 Wall Street, Suite 100
New York, NY 10005-5480
(212) 422-5456
Web site: http://www.amergeog.org

Florida Museum of Natural History
University of Florida—Powell Hall
SW 34th Street and Hull Road
P.O. Box 112710
Gainesville, FL 32611-2710
Web site: http://www.flmnh.ufl.edu

Hakluyt Society
c/o The Map Library
British Library
96 Euston Road
London NW1 2DB
England

Web site: http://www.hakluyt.com

The Mariners' Museum
100 Museum Drive
Newport News, VA 23606
(757) 596-2222
Web site: http://www.mariner.org

Maritime Park Association
P.O. Box 470310
San Francisco, CA 94147-0310
(415) 561-6662
Web site: http://www.maritime.org

Web Sites

Due to the changing nature of Internet links, the Rosen Publishing Group, Inc., has developed an online list of Web sites related to the subject of this book. This site is updated regularly. Please use this link to access the list:

http://www.rosenlinks.com/lee/jupl/

FOR FURTHER READING

Carrion, Arturo Morales. *Puerto Rico: A Political and Cultural History*. New York: W.W. Norton & Co., Inc., 1983.

Cumming, William P., R. A. Skelton, and David B. Quinn. *The Discovery of North America*. New York: American Heritage Press, 1977.

Fuson, Robert H. *Juan Ponce de León and the Spanish Discovery of Puerto Rico and Florida*. Granville, OH: The McDonald & Woodward Publishing Company, 2000.

Harmon, Daniel E. *Juan Ponce de León and the Search for the Fountain of Youth*. Broomall, PA: Chelsea House, 2000.

Peck, Douglas T. *Ponce de León and the Discovery of Florida*. St. Paul, MN: Pogo Press, 1993.

Peterson, Mendel. *The Funnel of Gold*. Boston: Little, Brown & Co., 1975.

BIBLIOGRAPHY

Cumming, William P., R. A. Skelton, and David B. Quinn. *The Discovery of North America.* New York: American Heritage Press, 1977.

Fuson, Robert H. *Juan Ponce de León and the Spanish Discovery of Puerto Rico and Florida.* Granville, OH: The McDonald & Woodward Publishing Company, 2000.

Morison, Samuel Eliot. *The Great Explorers.* New York: Oxford University Press, 1978.

Paiewonsky, Michael. *Conquest of Eden 1493–1515.* Rome: Mapes Monde Editore, 1991.

Peterson, Mendel L. *The Funnel of Gold.* Boston: Little, Brown & Co., 1975.

Sauer, Carl Ortwin. *The Early Spanish Main.* Berkeley, CA: University of California Press, 1992.

Van Middeldyk, R. A. *The History of Puerto Rico From the Spanish Discovery to the American Occupation.* New York: D. Appleton & Co., 1903.

INDEX

Index